Mastering GPTs:

A Comprehensive

Guide To

Creation,

Utilization,

And Monetization

Milena Sladkova

First edition: November 2023
Cover: Milena Sladkova

Table of contents:

Disclaimer: The contents of this book are for informational purposes only and are not intended to provide legal, financial, or professional advice. The information provided is based on author's personal experience and research and should not be relied upon as a substitute for professional advice. Readers are encouraged to consult with a qualified professional regarding their specific circumstances before making any decisions. All the information and strategies presented in this book are accurate to the best of the author's knowledge at the time of writing. However, the online landscape is dynamic and subject to constant change. Laws, regulations, and online platforms can evolve, and what may have been effective or accurate at the time of writing may no longer be so in the future. The author and publisher disclaim any liability arising directly or indirectly from the use of the information in this book.

Chapter 1:

Introduction to GPTs

Let's talk about GPTs. What are GPTs? How to create one? How to tailor them to your own liking? How to leverage this opportunity to generate income? These are all topics we are going to discuss in this book.

Simply, Generative Pre-trained Transformers or GPTs are custom made chats that tend to solve diverse range of problems, assist with learning a language, become your content creator, or they can be whatever you want them to be.

In recent years, revolutionary language models have transformed the way we interact with technology and opened up new avenues for creativity and problem-solving.

Embarking on a brief journey through the evolution of language models, from traditional rule-based systems to machine learning, and finally, the emergence of pre-trained transformers, the landscape has evolved significantly.

What makes GPTs stand out in the crowded space of language models? Their ability to understand context, generate coherent text, and easily be custom trained to perform various tasks.

GPTs can be used in diverse fields such as content creation, customer support, coding assistance, and much more. The real-world applications might surprise you!

GPTs are not just tools for experts; they're here to democratize AI, putting powerful language models in the hands of creators, thinkers, and problem solvers like you.

Before we dive deeper, let's explore why you should be excited about GPTs. Whether you're a developer, a content creator, or someone with a specific problem to solve, there's a place for you in the GPT revolution.

As we journey through this guide, we'll demystify the world of GPTs step by step. From understanding the core principles to creating your custom GPT, you'll gain the knowledge and skills to leverage the full potential of these language models.

Are you ready to embark on a transformative adventure with GPTs? Let's dive in!

Chapter 2:

Unveiling the Power of GPTs

Generative Pre-trained Transformers, commonly known as GPTs, have emerged as a game-changer in the realm of artificial intelligence. In this chapter, we'll delve deeper into what makes GPTs unique, exploring their architecture, capabilities, and real-world applications.

Understanding GPT Architecture

At the heart of GPTs lies a sophisticated architecture that enables them to comprehend and generate human-like text. These models, based on transformer architecture, consist of attention mechanisms that allow them to weigh the importance of different words in a sentence, capturing contextual relationships.

The transformer model is pre-trained on vast amounts of diverse text data, acquiring language patterns, grammar, and contextual understanding. This pre-training phase equips GPTs with a broad knowledge base, making them versatile in handling a myriad of tasks.

Core Capabilities of GPTs

GPTs boast several key capabilities that set them apart:

1. Contextual Understanding

Unlike traditional language models, GPTs understand context, ensuring that the generated text is coherent and contextually relevant. This contextual awareness enables them to produce more human-like responses.

2. Creative Text Generation

GPTs excel in creative text generation, from writing compelling stories to generating code snippets. Their ability to mimic human language makes them powerful tools for content creation.

3. Adaptability to Tasks

One remarkable aspect of GPTs is their ability to adapt to various tasks without task-specific training. From language translation to summarization, GPTs showcase a remarkable capacity to handle diverse challenges.

4. Problem-Solving Skills

GPTs can be applied as problem-solving tools, providing insights, suggestions, and solutions across different topics. Their versatility makes them valuable assets for both professionals and hobbyists.

Real-World Applications

The impact of GPTs extends far beyond theoretical concepts. They have found applications in:

Content Creation

GPTs play a pivotal role in supporting content creators throughout their creative journey. Specifically designed to assist in various aspects of content creation, these powerful models offer substantial benefits in generating diverse forms of written content, such as blog posts, articles, and creative pieces.

1. Content Generation:

GPTs excel in generating high-quality content, providing content creators with a versatile tool to streamline their writing process. Whether you're in need of compelling blog posts, informative articles, or imaginative pieces, GPTs are adept at producing coherent and contextually relevant text.

2. Idea Generation:

Beyond merely crafting sentences, GPTs serve as valuable collaborators during the ideation phase. Content creators can leverage these models to brainstorm fresh perspectives, innovative ideas, and unique angles for their projects. The ability to explore various concepts and themes makes GPTs an invaluable resource in the creative process.

3. Enhanced Creativity:

GPTs contribute to the enhancement of creativity by offering novel suggestions and contributing to the expansion of creative thinking. Their capacity to understand and mimic human-like language allows content creators to break through creative blocks and explore uncharted territories in their work.

4. Efficiency in Ideation:

The speed and efficiency with which GPTs operate make them particularly advantageous during the initial stages of ideation. Content creators can quickly receive a multitude of ideas, enabling them to refine and build upon these concepts, ultimately saving time and fostering a more productive creative workflow.

5. Diverse Applications:

GPTs are not limited to a specific niche; they adapt to the requirements of content creators across various industries. Whether you're a blogger, journalist, or fiction writer, GPTs offer a flexible solution to meet your specific content generation needs.

In essence, GPTs function as dynamic and innovative collaborators, providing content creators with the support they need to transform ideas into well-crafted, engaging content. As technology continues to evolve, GPTs stand at the forefront, redefining the creative landscape and empowering content creators to reach new heights in their work.

Coding Assistance

GPTs have emerged as indispensable assets in software development, acting as invaluable coding companions for developers seeking enhanced productivity and efficiency. Their versatile capabilities extend across various facets of the coding process, making them a go-to resource for developers looking to streamline their workflow.

1. Code Generation:

One of the primary applications of GPTs in the coding landscape is their ability to generate code snippets. Developers can articulate their coding needs, whether it's for a specific algorithm, function, or logic and GPTs respond by providing relevant and syntactically correct code segments. This feature significantly accelerates the coding process, especially during the initial stages of project development.

2. Debugging Assistance:

GPTs function as effective debugging companions, offering assistance in identifying and resolving coding errors. Developers can describe the issues they are facing, and GPTs, drawing on their extensive training data, provide insights into potential solutions, helping to troubleshoot and refine the code.

3. Algorithmic Support:

For developers grappling with complex algorithms or seeking optimization strategies, GPTs serve as knowledgeable aides. By articulating their algorithmic requirements, developers can receive guidance on structuring algorithms, optimizing code for performance, and exploring alternative approaches.

4. Code Refactoring Suggestions:

GPTs contribute to code quality by offering suggestions for refactoring. Developers can describe the specific functionality they aim to achieve, and GPTs, leveraging their understanding of coding best practices, propose improvements and optimizations to the existing codebase.

5. Learning and Skill Enhancement:

GPTs serve as valuable tools for developers looking to enhance their coding skills. Novice developers can seek guidance on coding principles, syntax, and best practices, while experienced developers can use GPTs to explore advanced concepts and stay updated on the latest coding trends.

6. Adaptability to Programming Languages:

GPTs are capable of providing assistance across a wide array of programming languages. This adaptability makes them a versatile companion for developers working in diverse coding environments.

In essence, GPTs have become integral members of the coding community, offering support at every stage of the development lifecycle. As coding companions, GPTs empower developers to overcome challenges, improve code quality, and foster continuous learning, ultimately contributing to a more efficient and dynamic software development process.

Customer Support

GPTs revolutionize the landscape of customer support by seamlessly integrating advanced language understanding capabilities into the interaction process. As adept conversational agents, GPTs play a pivotal role in enhancing customer satisfaction through quick, accurate, and context-aware responses to user queries. Here's an in-depth exploration of how GPTs contribute to the realm of customer support:

1. Natural Language Understanding:

GPTs are designed to comprehend and interpret natural language, allowing them to understand user queries in a manner that closely mirrors human conversation. This natural language processing (NLP) capability enables GPTs to capture the nuances and context of customer inquiries, laying the foundation for precise and contextually relevant responses.

2. Prompt and Efficient Responses:

Customer support often demands swift responses, and GPTs excel in providing timely answers to user questions. Whether addressing product-related queries, troubleshooting issues, or offering general assistance, GPTs leverage their vast knowledge base to generate prompt and accurate replies, contributing to a more efficient support process.

3. Context Retention:

GPTs showcase an impressive ability to retain context throughout a conversation. This means that they can comprehend follow-up questions and reference information from previous interactions, creating a more personalized and coherent dialogue. This contextual awareness contributes significantly to user satisfaction as customers feel understood and valued.

4. Handling Diverse Queries:

Customer support encompasses a wide array of queries, ranging from straightforward information requests to complex problem-solving. GPTs exhibit versatility in handling this diversity, capable of addressing inquiries related to product features, order status, account management, and more. Their adaptability positions them as valuable assets for comprehensive customer support coverage.

5. 24/7 Availability:

GPTs operate tirelessly, offering a round-the-clock support presence. This continuous availability ensures that customers can receive assistance whenever they require it, irrespective of time zones or business hours. The instantaneous nature of GPT responses contributes to a positive user experience and fosters customer loyalty.

6. Language Flexibility:

GPTs are not confined to a specific language or dialect, making them versatile in catering to a global customer base. Their language flexibility allows businesses to provide multilingual support effortlessly, accommodating users from diverse linguistic backgrounds.

7. Continuous Learning and Improvement:

GPTs learn from each customer interaction, continuously improving their ability to provide accurate and relevant responses. As they accumulate more data and feedback, GPTs refine their understanding of user queries, ensuring a progressive enhancement in the quality of customer support over time.

In summary, GPTs elevate customer support by embodying a fusion of linguistic prowess and technological efficiency. Their natural language understanding, context retention, and adaptability empower businesses to offer a sophisticated and user-centric support experience, ultimately fostering stronger customer relationships.

Language Translation

GPTs, with their language capabilities, play a pivotal role in breaking down language barriers and fostering global communication. Here's a closer look at how GPTs contribute to language translation tasks:

1. Seamless Multilingual Communication:

GPTs act as seamless intermediaries, effortlessly translating text from one language to another. This functionality is particularly valuable in diverse, multicultural settings where effective communication is of greatest importance. Users can input text in their preferred language, and GPTs ensure that the message is conveyed accurately and contextually in the desired language.

2. Preserving Context and Nuances:

What sets GPTs apart in language translation is their ability to preserve the context and nuances of the original text. Unlike conventional translation tools that may struggle with idiomatic expressions or cultural references, GPTs excel in capturing the subtleties of language, ensuring that the translated output maintains the intended meaning.

3. Enhancing Cross-Cultural Collaboration:

GPTs contribute to enhanced cross-cultural collaboration by enabling individuals who speak different languages to collaborate seamlessly. Whether it's in business, academia, or creative pursuits, GPTs facilitate effective communication, fostering collaboration on a global scale.

4. Efficient Content Localization:

Businesses expanding into new markets benefit from GPTs in efficiently localizing their content. GPTs not only translate the text but also assist in adapting it to the cultural nuances and preferences of the target audience. This ensures that the content resonates effectively with diverse audiences, contributing to the success of global ventures.

In summary, the language-agnostic nature of GPTs positions them as powerful allies in the realm of language translation, promoting understanding, collaboration, and connectivity across linguistic boundaries.

The Democratization of AI

One of the most significant contributions of GPTs is the democratization of AI. These models empower individuals, regardless of their technical expertise, to harness the capabilities of advanced language models. The era of exclusive AI access is fading, giving way to a more inclusive and collaborative approach.

Chapter 3:

Crafting Your Own GPT

In this chapter, we'll explore the step-by-step process of crafting your personalized GPT, tailored to meet your specific needs. The process is very simple and requires two things from you: to have a great idea and to have the information related to this idea gathered into a PDF that you can upload and train you GPT on it.

Here's a step-by-step guide to creating your own GPT:

1. Navigate to https://chat.openai.com/gpts/editor or click on the "Explore Tab" and you will see "My GPTs".

2. Click on "Create a GPT" to initiate the process.

3. In the "Create Tab", interact with the GPT Builder by providing specific instructions. For instance, you can say, "Create a GPT that assists in generating keywords for new products" or "Develop a GPT with the skills of a software engineer for code formatting."

4. Move to the "Configure Tab" to name your GPT and define its description. Here, you can also choose the actions your GPT will perform, such as web browsing or image creation.

5. Once satisfied, click "Publish" to make your GPT accessible. You can also share it with others if you want.

Congratulations! You have successfully created your own GPT.

The Publish button has three different options:

Only me: for your own use only.

Only people with a link: share a link with your friends and colleagues to use your custom GPT.

Public: make it available to anyone. If it qualifies for the GPT store you can earn profit if people search and use your GPT (agent).

Advanced Settings in the "Configure Tab"

Within the GPT Editor, you have the ability to fine-tune and customize detailed settings for your GPT.

Follow these steps for advanced configuration:

1. Navigate the Tabs:

At the top of the GPT Editor, you'll find two tabs named Create and Configure. The "Create Tab" lets you interact with the GPT Builder for general instructions, while the "Configure Tab" allows you to provide more specific and detailed instructions.

2. "Configure Tab" Settings:

Adding Images: Request the GPT Builder to generate an image or upload your own by accessing the "Configure Tab". When you create your GPT, the builder will ask you if you want it to create the Profile picture for you. You can try several options until you get one that you like. You can always replace it later with your own design if you wish.

Additional Instructions: Provide in-depth instructions and guidelines regarding the GPT's behavior, functionalities, and any specific behaviors to avoid. The bot will ask you how you want your GPT to behave and interact. Here you can provide it with specific instructions, for example, what tone to use or which topics to avoid.

Prompt Starters: Explore examples of prompts that users can initiate to start a conversation. You can think of good ideas that would the users of your custom GPT want to ask first. The bot will offer you some ideas, you can simply change them by clicking the X (deleting them) and adding your own.

Knowledge: Furnish additional context for your GPT by uploading files. Note that the content from these files will be included in the GPT's output. This is a very important function of GPT. The knowledge of ChatGPT is not current, but always at least a year behind on information. What you can do here is, gather all the new and relevant information regarding your custom GPT and upload it as PDFs. The bot will read these files, update its information and provide it to the people who use your GPT. This is how you **train** your GPT.

Gathering Data: Start by collecting comprehensive and reliable information related to your chosen GPT topic. Whether it's recent industry trends, user preferences, or specialized knowledge, an extensive dataset is the backbone of an effective GPT.

Uploading Data as PDF: Once you've compiled the data, organize it into a PDF format. This ensures that the information is structured, accessible, and easily integrated into the GPT. The "Configure Tab" serves as the repository for this uploaded data, becoming the knowledge base that your GPT draws upon to deliver informed responses.

By meticulously curating and uploading data, you enhance your GPT's capabilities, enabling it to offer meaningful insights and guidance. The quality of the data you provide directly influences the effectiveness of your GPT, making the process of data collection and upload a pivotal aspect of your journey to GPT success.

New Capabilities: Enable functionalities like Web Browsing, DALL·E Image Generation, and Advanced Data Analysis for expanded capabilities. After enabling these in the "Configure Tab" your bot will be much more capable of analysing data and provinding more accurate and helpful answers.

Custom Actions: Zapier AI Actions can integrate third-party APIs into your GPT by specifying details about endpoints, parameters, and how the model should utilize them. You can import actions from an OpenAPI schema, making it compatible with existing plugins. You need to sign up also with Zapier AI Actions so that you are able to use this function. Basically, the GPT can be connected to the real world, for example, to read and answer emails, send messages through private chat, etc. On the Zapier page, you will find detailed instructions on how to integrate the Actions into your GPT. Once integrated, you will need to log in to the Action you want to use in your GPT and allow permissions; otherwise, you won't be able to test it out.

Use these advanced settings to tailor your GPT to meet specific requirements and enhance its performance.

If you encounter any access issues, ensure that you've enabled **BETA features** and upgraded your plan to **GPT-4 Plus**. You can enable Beta features in the left-down corner of your screen. Click on your name; go to Settings & Beta, click Beta features, and allow Beta settings.

Chapter 4:

Helpful Steps

Choosing a Purpose

Defining the purpose of your GPT is akin to setting the compass for a grand journey; it directs the entire trajectory of your creation. The profound impact your GPT can have is intimately tied to the clarity with which you articulate its purpose.

Crafting a Purposeful GPT for Content Creation:

If your GPT is geared towards aiding content creation, envision it as a virtual muse, poised to inspire and generate captivating narratives. Consider the tone, style, and themes it should encapsulate. Whether you're delving into blog posts, articles, or creative pieces, a well-defined purpose ensures that your GPT becomes an indispensable companion for content creators seeking fresh ideas and eloquent expressions.

Empowering Developers with Coding Assistance:

For those channeling their GPT's prowess into coding assistance, the purpose takes on a technical essence. Your GPT becomes a coding companion, adept at generating snippets, assisting in debugging, and streamlining the coding process. Clearly outlining the coding languages, frameworks, and functionalities your GPT should support sets the stage for a seamless integration into the developer's toolkit.

Knowledge-Centric GPTs:

In scenarios where the emphasis is on providing specific knowledge, the purpose becomes an intellectual beacon. Envisage your GPT as a virtual expert, ready to answer queries, provide insights, and serve as a repository of information. Define the scope of knowledge it should encompass, ensuring that users find reliable and accurate responses to their inquiries.

The Clarity-Power Nexus:

The power of your GPT lies in the precision with which its purpose is defined. A clear purpose not only streamlines its capabilities but also resonates with users, creating a distinct niche in the expansive landscape of AI. It transforms your GPT from a generic tool into a purposeful solution, tailored to meet specific needs and challenges.

User-Centric Innovation:

As you delve into defining your GPT's purpose, keep the end-user in sharp focus. Anticipate their needs, understand their pain points, and tailor your GPT to be a solution that seamlessly integrates into their workflows. The purpose-driven design is not just a technical consideration; it's a user-centric innovation that elevates your GPT from a mere tool to a transformative asset.

In essence, the journey of defining your GPT's purpose is a voyage of intentionality. It's about imbuing your creation with a sense of mission, aligning its capabilities with the real-world problems it seeks to solve. As the architect of this virtual entity, your ability to articulate a purpose that resonates is the cornerstone of unlocking the true potential of your GPT.

Naming Your GPT

Naming your GPT is not a mere formality; it's an opportunity to infuse character and purpose into its digital existence. Consider it akin to naming a business or a beloved pet. The chosen name should resonate with the essence of what your GPT embodies. If it's a coding companion, the name might evoke efficiency and precision, while a content creation assistant could sport a name exuding creativity and inspiration. A purposeful name serves as the beacon for users, guiding them towards the GPT's intended role and functionalities.

Establishing a Connection:

Just as a well-named pet becomes an integral part of a family, a well-named GPT establishes a connection with its users. It transforms the interaction from a sterile engagement with technology to a more personalized and relatable experience. Users should feel a sense of familiarity and comfort when interfacing with your creation. The right name can turn your GPT into more than a tool; it becomes a trusted companion in the digital realm.

Designing an AI Profile

In the vast digital landscape, where interactions are often limited to text, introducing a visual element to your GPT can be a game-changer. The ability to customize your GPT's appearance, akin to giving it a distinct face, provides a visual identity that resonates with users. Much like a logo for a brand, the AI profile picture becomes the face of your creation.

Why Customize?

Customization goes beyond mere aesthetics; it reinforces the uniqueness of your GPT. The generated AI profile picture serves as a visual representation of your creation's persona and purpose. A coding companion, it might feature elements associated with programming, creating an instant connection for users seeking coding assistance. On the other hand, a content creation assistant's profile picture could exude creativity, aligning with its role in generating innovative ideas.

Easier Recognition:

In a world flowing with information, a visually distinct AI profile picture aids in instant recognition. Users can quickly identify and associate with your GPT in the crowded digital sphere. It's not just about making your creation visually appealing; it's about creating a visual brand that users can easily spot and remember.

The Power of Personalization:

Humans are inherently drawn to personalized experiences. Customizing your GPT's appearance is a step towards humanizing the interaction. Users are more likely to engage with a creation that feels unique and tailored to their needs. The AI profile picture becomes a visual cue, signaling that this GPT is designed to cater to specific requirements.

Configuring Information

The pre-trained capabilities of GPTs lay a robust foundation, but fine-tuning their knowledge base is the key to unlocking their full potential. Incorporating relevant data serves as a dynamic supplement, ensuring that your GPT stays in tune with the ever-evolving landscape of information.

The Power of Relevance:

In a world where information evolves rapidly, relevance is paramount. Fine-tuning your GPT with the latest data sharpens its responses and recommendations, aligning them with current trends, industry insights, and user expectations. Whether your GPT is assisting with coding or content creation, relevance ensures that it remains a valuable and up-to-date resource.

Adaptability to Trends:

Trends come and go, and user preferences shift. A GPT armed with recent data can navigate these changes effectively. For instance, a content creation GPT tuned into the latest industry developments can generate content that aligns with current trends, enhancing its usefulness for creators seeking cutting-edge insights.

How to Fine-Tune:

Fine-tuning involves updating your GPT's knowledge base by incorporating specific datasets. This can range from industry reports and articles to user-generated content, depending on your GPT's purpose. Uploading this data ensures that your GPT becomes a reliable source of information that resonates with users seeking the latest and most pertinent insights.

Ensuring Accuracy:

The reliability of your GPT hinges on the accuracy of its information. Fine-tuning acts as a quality control mechanism, refining the GPT's responses to be not only relevant but also accurate. Users relying on your GPT for coding advice or content creation expect precision, and fine-tuning is the tool that ensures your GPT meets these expectations.

Continuous Improvement:

Knowledge refinement is an ongoing process. Regularly updating and fine-tuning your GPT's knowledge base ensures its longevity and continued effectiveness. It positions your creation as a trusted companion that evolves with the times, making it an indispensable tool for users across various domains.

Refining Instructions

Specify how your GPT should present information and interact with users. Tailor the tone, style, and level of detail to match the preferences and needs of your target audience.

Understanding Your Audience:

Begin by comprehending the demographics, preferences, and expectations of your target audience. Are they seeking formal and detailed responses, or do they prefer a more casual and concise interaction? By aligning your GPT's communication style with the audience's preferences, you enhance the overall user experience.

Adapt Tone and Style:

Consider the context in which your GPT will be employed. Whether it's a professional setting, educational platform, or casual conversational use, adapting the tone and style accordingly is vital. A GPT assisting in academic research might adopt a more formal tone, while a creative writing companion could be more expressive and imaginative.

Fine-Tune Level of Detail:

Recognize the importance of providing information at an appropriate level of detail. Some users may appreciate in-depth explanations, while others prefer succinct responses. Striking the right balance ensures that your GPT caters to a diverse audience, making it versatile across various applications.

Feedback Mechanism:

Implement a robust feedback mechanism to gather insights into user satisfaction and areas for improvement. Regularly evaluate and adjust the GPT's interaction parameters based on user feedback, fostering an iterative process of refinement.

Avoiding Pitfalls

As you embark on the journey of creating your GPT, it's crucial to provide clear guidance on areas to avoid. This strategic step serves as a safeguard, preventing unintended outcomes and ensuring that the generated content remains aligned with your intended purpose. Here's a brief exploration of why and how to set boundaries for your GPT:

Maintaining Purposeful Content:

By delineating areas to avoid, you establish a framework that directs the GPT toward generating content that is purposeful, relevant, and aligned with your defined objectives. This clarity helps in steering the GPT away from producing content that might deviate from the intended use.

Preventing Misinformation:

In the age of information, accuracy is a must. Clearly indicating what your GPT should refrain from ensures that it doesn't propagate misinformation or create content that might confuse users. This preventive measure contributes to maintaining trust and credibility.

Enhancing User Experience:

Setting boundaries is not just about limitations; it's about enhancing the overall user experience. Users interact with your GPT with certain expectations, and by guiding the model away from certain topics or styles, you create a more controlled and tailored experience.

Mitigating Ethical Concerns:

Ethical considerations have a very important role in AI development. By instructing your GPT on areas to avoid, you proactively address potential ethical pitfalls. This proactive approach aligns with responsible AI practices, showcasing your commitment to ethical content generation.

Testing and Iterating

Before releasing your GPT into the world, it's imperative to undergo thorough testing. This critical phase involves evaluating various aspects of your creation, from design to functionality, to ensure it aligns seamlessly with your vision. Here's a deeper dive into the importance of testing and the iterative process of refining your GPT:

Ensuring Alignment with Vision:

Testing serves as a litmus test to verify whether your GPT aligns with the envisioned purpose. By subjecting it to real-world scenarios and diverse inputs, you can identify areas where adjustments are necessary to better achieve your intended goals.

Iterating on Design:

The testing phase allows you to gather valuable insights into the user experience and interaction dynamics. Pay attention to user feedback and iterate on the design accordingly. This could involve tweaking the interface, refining the visual elements, or enhancing the overall usability to create a more intuitive and user-friendly GPT.

Fine-Tuning Instructions:

Instructions play a pivotal role in shaping your GPT's behavior. Testing provides an opportunity to assess how well the model interprets and executes instructions. If certain aspects of your GPT's responses or actions need improvement, refining the instructions becomes a key part of the iterative process.

Knowledge Base Enhancement:

Evaluate the effectiveness of your GPT's knowledge base during testing. Identify areas where additional information or updates are required to ensure the model stays current and relevant. This step is crucial for enhancing the GPT's overall performance and its ability to generate accurate and up-to-date content.

Optimizing for Performance:

Testing helps identify potential bottlenecks or performance issues. Whether it is response time, resource utilization, or other technical considerations, optimizing your GPT for peak performance ensures a smoother and more efficient user experience.

User Feedback Integration:

Actively seek feedback from users during the testing phase. User insights are invaluable for understanding how people interact with your GPT and what improvements can be made. Incorporating user feedback into your refinement process enhances the user-centric nature of your creation.

Iterative Refinement:

Refinement is an iterative process. Based on the findings from testing, make informed adjustments to your GPT's design, instructions, and knowledge base. This continuous cycle of refinement ensures that your GPT evolves and improves over time, staying attuned to user needs and expectations.

Unleashing the Power of Your GPT

Once your GPT is configured to your satisfaction, it's ready to assist and engage with users. Whether you aim to simplify content creation, streamline coding processes, or offer valuable insights, your personalized GPT is a testament to the democratization of AI.

Chapter 5:

Finding Your Perfect GPT Idea

In the vast landscape of possibilities, choosing the right idea for your GPT can be an exciting yet challenging journey. Here, we'll explore ten potential GPT concepts that cater to diverse needs, providing a launching pad for your creative exploration.

1. Content Creation Companion:

Unlock the doors to creativity with a GPT designed to assist users in generating compelling content. Tailor-made for writers, graphic designers, or video producers, this GPT can offer valuable suggestions for captivating headlines, engaging introductions, and powerful conclusions. Imagine the possibilities as your GPT becomes a trusted ally in the creative process.

2. Code Optimization Guru:

For the coding enthusiasts, envision a GPT that goes beyond syntax checks. A Code Optimization Guru can provide real-time debugging assistance, recommend efficient coding practices, and introduce developers to relevant libraries or frameworks. Streamline the coding experience and enhance the quality of software projects with this specialized GPT.

3. Learning Language Mentor:

Breaking language barriers becomes seamless with a GPT that doubles as a Learning Language Mentor. Offering conversational practice, grammar corrections, and vocabulary expansion, this GPT caters to language learners at various proficiency levels. Personalized lessons make language acquisition an enjoyable and effective experience.

4. Personalized Fitness Coach:

Step into the realm of health and wellness by creating a GPT that serves as a Personalized Fitness Coach. Tailor workouts to individual fitness goals, consider preferences and health constraints and provide nutritional advice. Witness the transformation as users embark on their fitness journey with guidance from your GPT.

5. Financial Planning Advisor:

Guide users toward financial success with a GPT that specializes in Financial Planning. From budgeting to investment decisions, this GPT offers insights into market trends and potential opportunities. Empower individuals to make informed financial choices and navigate the complexities of personal finance.

6. Social Media Manager Assistant:

Empower users to conquer the social media landscape with a GPT designed as a Social Media Manager Assistant. From content ideas to optimal posting times, this GPT aids in managing social media presence. Track analytics and receive actionable insights for improving engagement and reach.

7. Health and Wellness Companion:

Prioritize well-being with a GPT functioning as a Health and Wellness Companion. Provide mental health support, stress management tips, and mindfulness exercises. Share information on healthy recipes and nutritional advice, fostering holistic health and balance.

8. Job Application Strategist:

Navigate the competitive job market with a GPT that serves as a Job Application Strategist. Craft personalized resumes and cover letters, prepare for interviews and strategize for career advancement. Empower job seekers with the tools they need to stand out in the professional realm.

9. Virtual Travel Guide:

Bring the world to users' fingertips with a GPT designed as a Virtual Travel Guide. Plan personalized travel itineraries based on preferences, budget, and interests. Offer insights into local cultures, traditions, and must-visit attractions, creating unforgettable travel experiences.

10. Innovative Business Idea Generator:

Unleash entrepreneurial potential with a GPT functioning as an Innovative Business Idea Generator. Explore unique and viable business concepts aligned with market trends, user interests, and emerging technologies. Provide insights into target audiences and effective marketing strategies.

Cultivating Your Unique GPT Idea:

While these GPT concepts serve as a starting point, the true magic lies in your creativity. Consider your passions, expertise, and the unique problems you want to solve. Your GPT has the potential to revolutionize the way users interact with technology, so let your imagination run wild. Remember, the most successful GPTs often emerge from the intersection of innovation, utility, and a deep understanding of user needs. Your journey toward creating a groundbreaking GPT begins with the seed of your own inventive spirit.

To achieve success with your GPT, a critical step involves training it with relevant and up-to-date data. This process ensures that your GPT is well-equipped to provide accurate and valuable information to users. If you don't already possess the necessary data, the "Configure Tab" in the GPT creator becomes your ally.

Conclusion:

Monetizing the Potential of GPTs

In the dynamic landscape of artificial intelligence, Generative Pre-trained Transformers (GPTs) stand not only as technological marvels but as gateways to lucrative opportunities. As we traverse the chapters of this guide, we've uncovered the foundational elements of GPTs, unraveling the multitude of ways these powerful tools can be harnessed to not just fuel creativity but also to generate revenue.

From being indispensable collaborators for content creators and developers to revolutionizing customer support and language translation, GPTs emerge as valuable assets in the pursuit of financial success. The breadth of their applications spans industries, offering a canvas for lucrative endeavors limited only by your imagination.

As you embark on the journey of creating a GPT, recognize that beyond the realm of technological innovation lies a landscape ripe with monetary potential. GPTs can be crafted and fine-tuned to cater to market demands, whether as content generators, coding assistants, or multilingual communicators. The customization options, advanced configurations, and detailed settings empower you to not only meet personal objectives but to tap into profitable niches.

In the realm of GPTs, the fusion of creativity and commerce becomes apparent. Your GPT is not merely a creation; it's a marketable solution to real-world challenges. The avenues for monetization are diverse, ranging from selling access to your

GPT's capabilities to offering specialized services that cater to specific industries.

As you navigate the landscape of GPTs, seize the opportunity to turn your creation into a revenue stream. Whether you envision your GPT as a subscription-based service, a consulting tool, or a key player in automated content generation for businesses, the potential for financial success is yours to explore.

Monetizing the potential of GPTs is not just a prospect; it's a reality waiting to be shaped by your entrepreneurial spirit. The collaborative potential of GPTs extends beyond personal use, inviting you to participate in a marketplace hungry for innovative solutions. Your GPT, when strategically positioned and marketed, can be a source of not just technological pride but also financial reward.

May your exploration of GPTs be not only a journey of discovery and innovation but a pathway to financial prosperity. Unleash the power of GPTs, harness their marketable potential, and let your entrepreneurial endeavors flourish in the lucrative realm of artificial intelligence. The future is yours to shape, and with a monetized GPT, the possibilities are boundless.

More from this author:

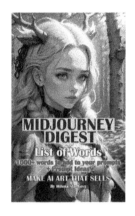

MIDJOURNEY DIGEST:

Make AI Art That Sells: **List of Words** 1000+ *words to add to your prompts* + Prompt Ideas

www.ingramcontent.com/pod-product-compliance
Lightning Source LLC
LaVergne TN
LVHW041222050326
832903LV00021B/743